PRESENTED BY

Michael Moulton
in honor of
Mrs. Addicks, 2nd Grade

SMYTHE GAMBRELL
LIBRARY

I love books

WESTMINSTER SCHOOLS

Science Experiments

ENERGY

by
John Farndon

BENCHMARK BOOKS

MARSHALL CAVENDISH
NEW YORK

Marshall Cavendish Corporation

99 White Plains Road

Tarrytown, New York 10591

© Marshall Cavendish Corporation, 2003

Created by Brown Partworks Limited

Library of Congress Cataloging-in-Publication Data

Farndon, John

  Energy / by John Farndon
    p. cm. — (Science experiments)
Includes index.
  ISBN 0-7614-1469-X
Summary: Discussion of, and experiments supporting, scientific properties
and principles of energy
  1. Force and energy—Juvenile literature. 2. Power
(Mechanics)—Experiments—Juvenile literature. [1. Force and
energy—Experiments. 2. Power (Mechanics)—Experiments. 3.
Experiments.] I. Title. II. Series.

  QC73.4 .F37 2003
  531'.6'078—dc21

                                                    2002004631

Printed in Hong Kong

PHOTOGRAPHIC CREDITS

Corbis: p11, Karl Weatherby; p14, Milepost 92; p18, Peter Johnson; p20,
Jenny Muench; p21, Georgia Lowell
Duracell PLC: p7
Enron Wind Power: p28/29
Image Bank: p12, Derek P Redfern; p24, Sean Justice Productions; p28,
Harald Sund
NASA: pp16/17, JJ Hester, Arizona State Library
National Archery: p8
Pictor International: p4, p6, p25, p26
Sandia National: p22
Stanford Linear: p5

Step-by-step photography throughout: Martin Norris

Front cover: Enron Wind Power

Contents

WHAT IS ENERGY?

Energy is one of the most important things in the universe. Without energy, nothing would happen, anywhere, at any time. Energy is involved in every movement in the universe, from the whirling of a huge galaxy to the tiny vibrations of an atom. Energy fuels the stars and keeps them shining brightly.

Down on Earth, energy lights our cities. It powers cars, trains, planes, and boats. It keeps factories going. It makes plants grow and fruit ripen. It keeps homes warm, and cooks food. It makes music, pictures on the television, and moving games on a computer. Every living body from bacteria to humans is kept going by energy.

The bright lights, moving cars and buses, and heat of the city use huge amounts of energy.

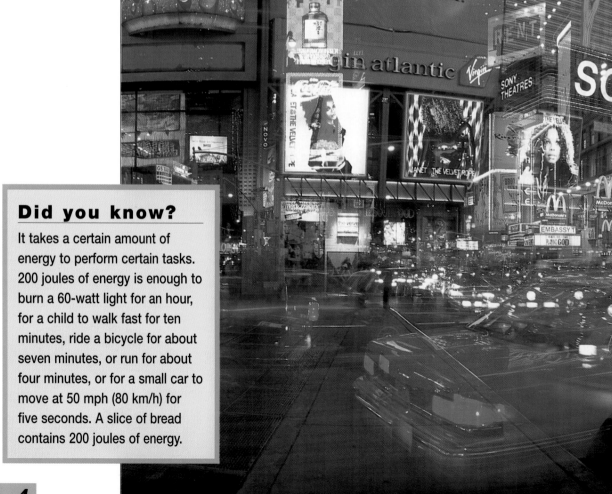

Did you know?

It takes a certain amount of energy to perform certain tasks. 200 joules of energy is enough to burn a 60-watt light for an hour, for a child to walk fast for ten minutes, ride a bicycle for about seven minutes, or run for about four minutes, or for a small car to move at 50 mph (80 km/h) for five seconds. A slice of bread contains 200 joules of energy.

MEASURING ENERGY

One way to measure energy is to find out how far it can move a certain weight. A joule is the amount of energy it takes to lift one pound up nine inches. Another way is to measure how much energy heats something up. A British thermal unit, or Btu, is the energy it takes to raise the temperature of one pound of water by 1°F. 1 Btu equals 1,000 joules.

Every particle in the universe is concentrated energy. This machine, called a calorimeter, shows that even the tiniest particle contains large amounts.

Scientists define energy simply as the "capacity to do work." Work is really another word for making something change. So energy is the power to change something—typically by heating it up or making it move. Water is changed to steam when it is heated up, for example; the heat is energy.

Energy comes in many forms. Heat is a form of energy, called thermal energy. Light is a form of energy, too, called radiant energy. Electricity is also energy. Mechanical energy is the energy of physical movement, like a person running or machine turning. Chemical energy is the energy stored within chemicals. Other forms of energy include solar energy (the Sun's energy) and nuclear energy (the energy of atoms).

KINDS OF ENERGY

Energy is the power to make things happen. It can exist in two ways. It can be ready to make something happen. This is called stored, or potential, energy. Or it can actually be making something happen. This is called kinetic energy.

Whenever something happens, movement is involved. This is why kinetic energy is also called movement energy. It is the energy something has when it is moving. A moving bicycle has kinetic energy. So does a ball whizzing across the football field, or a speeding bullet, or a plummeting rock.

It is clear that a moving object has energy because of what happens when something gets

A sprinter's body is a powerhouse of potential energy, stored as chemicals in his muscles. As he moves off the block, his body converts this to kinetic, movement energy.

Did you know?

The human body might not seem that efficient at converting its stored energy to action. Yet a person could ride a bike for half an hour on the chemical energy stored in one candy bar. It takes the energy of 2,000 candy bars to heat up a pot of coffee!

in its way. The painful impact if someone is hit by a flying ball, a bicycle or, worse still, a bullet shows this energy dramatically.

The more massive an object is and the faster it is moving, the more kinetic energy it has. In fact, scientists have found there is a way of calculating kinetic energy. They simply halve the object's mass (its weight) and multiply this by its velocity, or speed, twice. This can be written as an equation:

$$E = \tfrac{1}{2}mv^2$$

Here m is the mass of the object, and v^2 is its speed multiplied by itself.

Stored or potential energy is less easy to appreciate. A stretched elastic band or a squeezed spring, for instance, have potential energy because they will spring back—and move—as soon as they're let go.

A ball held above the ground has potential energy, too, because it falls if let go. Once falling, the potential energy becomes kinetic energy. The ball held high has energy because it is affected by Earth's gravity. The higher it is held, the more strongly gravity pulls, and the greater potential energy the ball has. Anything high up and in a position to fall has this potential energy. Because it depends on gravity, this energy is called gravitational potential energy.

Batteries release stores of chemical energy to give electricity.

CHEMICAL ENERGY

It often takes energy, such as heat, to make chemical particles combine. But once joined, they have potential energy, just like a squeezed spring. This energy is released as soon as the bonds between chemicals are broken. Some chemicals, like sugars, are rich stores of energy. In "exothermic" chemical reactions, strong bonds break to release potential energy as heat. "Endothermic" reactions work the other way—taking heat from the surroundings to build strong bonds that are rich in potential energy.

With all these examples—the elastic band, spring, and ball— the potential energy does not come from nowhere. Energy has to be used to stretch the elastic band, squeeze the spring, and lift the ball. In fact, the amount of potential energy each gains is in direct proportion to the energy put in. The harder the band is stretched, the stronger the spring is squeezed, the higher the ball is lifted, the more potential energy each gains.

STORED ENERGY

You will need

- ✓ A trampoline of some kind, or simply a strong mattress you can safely jump on
- ✓ Yourself or a friend to jump on the trampoline

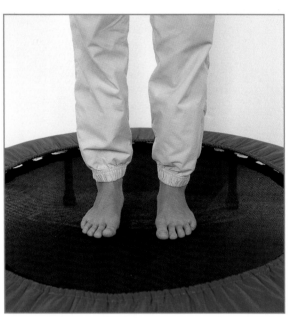

1 Stand on the trampoline. There is no energy but the potential energy stored in your muscles.

In the real world

ARCHERY

Archery depends on the buildup of potential energy in the bow's string as the archer pulls it back. When ready to fire, the archer lets the string go, and this energy is converted to kinetic energy in the arrow.

By pulling back slowly, an archer puts great potential energy in the bowstring.

3 Jump high into the air. The muscle energy you used to launch you is now converted to kinetic (movement) energy.

What is happening?

Bouncing on a trampoline involves a constant switching between stored, potential energy (PE) and kinetic, movement energy (KE). Chemical PE in your muscles is converted to KE as you leap up. At the top of your leap, the PE due to gravity pulls you down, giving you KE. As you hit the trampoline, the KE changes to PE in the trampoline as it stretches. This is given back to you as KE as you fly up again, aided by PE from your muscles.

2 Bend your knees, preparing to jump and begin to use muscle energy.

Keep on jumping up and down on the trampoline. You should find that as you go on jumping, you need less and less effort to jump—or you can jump much higher with the same effort. This is because each time you fall and hit the trampoline, the trampoline stretches down a little, because it is made of elastic material. It then bounces back, giving you a lift on the way. The higher you jump, the harder you hit the trampoline as you come down, and the more it stretches—and so the bigger the push it gives you on your way back up.

MOVEMENT ENERGY

You will need

✔ A simple swing, either with a seat or a rope with a knot

✔ Yourself, and perhaps a friend to push you

1 Sitting still on a swing, the only energy is potential—chemical in your muscles and gravitational from your weight.

What is happening?

To get a swing going, you use stored chemical energy in your muscles, swinging high to gain potential energy (PE) due to gravity. At the top of each swing, you have maximum PE. As you swing down, you lose PE, but gain kinetic, movement, energy (KE) as you move faster. The KE carries you up the other side. As you swing higher, you slow as KE is lost fighting gravity. Eventually all KE is gone, but you have gained PE from your height so you swing down, gaining KE again. So KE and PE alternate.

2 Bend your legs and start to swing back, by shifting your upper body weight forward.

3 Let yourself swing down by leaning back to shift your weight again.

In the real world

ENERGY IN SPORT

A sportsman uses stored, chemical energy from his muscles, but he learns to exploit gravitational potential energy (GPE) and kinetic energy. A cyclist can save on muscle energy by using GPE to speed him downhill, and KE on the flat.

Cyclists need high energy drinks to supply muscles.

5 Near the top of the swing, pull your upper body forward sharply and curl your legs under again.

4 As you pass the lowest point, lean back and stretch out your legs to help pull you forward.

Keep on repeating this sequence, swinging forward and backward to build up momentum. You will have to put quite a bit of effort in to start with—shifting your weight in an S-shape from head to toe and back again. But after a while you should be able to swing fast and freely with little effort.

ENERGY CHANGES

Energy comes in many forms, but it always works in two ways—energy transfer and energy conversion. Together these are called energy transformations.

Energy transfer simply means it moves from one place to another, as when smoke rises or a person kicks a ball. Energy conversion means changing from one form of energy to another. A dancer's muscles, for instance, convert chemical energy into movement.

Natural transformations are happening throughout the universe all the time, and they keep the universe going. But people also rely on energy transformations to give them energy in the right form.

Leaves are flat and wide to soak up as much energy from the Sun as they can. They use a green chemical called chlorophyll to convert this energy to sugar.

Did you know?

The leaves of plants are solar energy cells. They use sunlight to chemically join carbon dioxide gas from the air with water to make the energy-rich sugars plants need to grow. This process is called photosynthesis.

ENERGY CHAINS

All the energy in the universe has existed since the beginning of time. It simply changes from one form to another. The energy in even everyday events has always existed and always will. A TV's energy can be traced back through a series of conversions to light from the Sun, and the Sun's energy can be traced back to the dawn of the universe. Some of the Sun's energy was soaked up by leaves of plants living 300 million years ago. When the plants died, they were buried deep and squeezed into coal by accumulating layers of rock above, concentrating the energy. This coal is then mined from the ground and burned in a power station to boil water to steam and drive turbines, which generate electricity. The electricity is sent through wires to the TV. Similar chains of energy conversions occur for every bit of energy in the universe, stretching through all time.

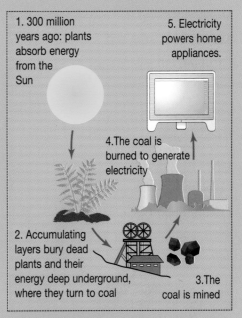

1. 300 million years ago: plants absorb energy from the Sun

2. Accumulating layers bury dead plants and their energy deep underground, where they turn to coal

3. The coal is mined

4. The coal is burned to generate electricity

5. Electricity powers home appliances.

The energy in coal that is burned to generate electricity comes originally from sunlight.

Mechanical energy can be converted to electrical energy by generators. As electricity, the energy is controllable, concentrated power for everything from trains to computers. Transformations ensure the energy is stored and delivered at the right time. A battery stores energy in chemical form then transforms it to electricity when needed.

It is not always possible to control when energy is transformed. An accidental explosion is the sudden transformation of chemical energy to heat energy.

PUTTING ENERGY TO WORK

You will need

- ✔ A 12-inch (30 cm) length of ⅛-inch (0.3 cm) copper tubing
- ✔ A craft knife
- ✔ Pliers or vise
- ✔ A pencil
- ✔ A tealight candle
- ✔ A rectangular piece of balsa wood, cut into a boat shape

1 Ask an adult to grip one end of the tube in a vise or pliers, then gradually bend the tube into a coil around a pencil.

In the real world

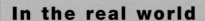

STEAM LOCOMOTIVES

Steam locomotives work by turning heat energy to mechanical energy. They burn coal in a firebox to heat up water in a boiler, making steam. The steam drives a piston to and fro; the piston turns the wheels via connecting rods and cranks.

Steam locomotives are heat engines.

3 Invert the boat, and bend the ends of the tube backward at about 45°. Clean the ends of the tube with a pin.

2 Place the candle on the balsa. Push the two ends of the tube right through the candle and the boat.

What is happening?

All engines work by converting one form of energy to another. Heat engines—powering everything from trucks to space rockets—use heat energy to drive mechanical movement. This boat is a simple form of heat engine. Here the heat source is the candle. The flame heats the water in the coil of the tube. The water gets so hot that it turns to steam. The steam swells out of the tube, pushing the boat forward. The steam condenses (turns to water), and more water is drawn back into the tube. The candle heats the water again, turning to steam and driving it from the tube. So the boat moves forward in a series of pulses.

Place one tube end with the opening up under the stream from a faucet and suck the other end like a straw to fill the tube with water. Hold the water in with your fingers while you push the whole boat underwater. Let the boat come up to the surface with the candle upward. Dab the candle dry, then ask an adult to light it. The boat should start to move slowly.

CONSERVING ENERGY

When someone is tired after a long run, they may say they've run out of energy. But the energy has not disappeared; it simply changed to heat as the runner's muscles burned sugar in their cells. This heat was left behind in the body, the air, and the ground, making all three slightly warmer.

It is impossible to destroy or create energy. It can only be moved or changed from one form to another. This is the law of Conservation of Energy. The total amount of energy after any change is always exactly the same as the total before. Energy is never really lost—it is just converted to another form.

Although energy is never lost it can be burned up. Every time energy is used, some is converted into heat. This is why light bulbs get hot and people get hot after exercise. Because heat energy spreads out thinly in all directions, it is very hard to use again. It is said to be dissipated, or less concentrated.

All engines driven by heat, such as steam engines and

In focus

THE LAWS OF THERMODYNAMICS

The movement of heat energy is called thermodynamics and it is governed by two key scientific laws. The first is similar to the Conservation of Energy law. It says that the total energy in the universe has been and always will be the same. The second says that some energy turns to heat every time energy changes. This may mean that all the universe ends up as nothing but heat.

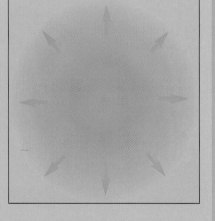

Heat spreads outward—from hot to cold—every time energy is converted or moves.

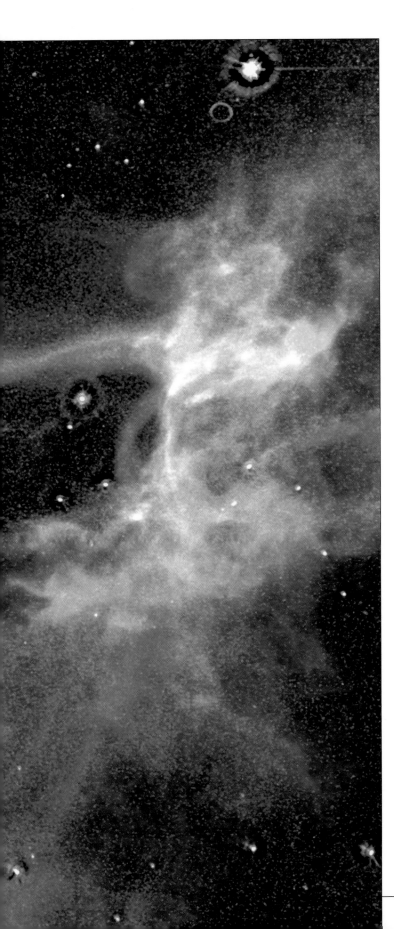

automobile engines, work because one part of the engine is hot and the other is cold. The flow of heat energy from hot to cold drives the engine.

The same principle is true in all energy changes. Whenever something happens, energy moves areas of high energy (or high temperature) to areas of lower energy. The movement is always from high to low.

A hot cup of soup left standing will gradually cool as its heat spreads into the surrounding air, warming the air slightly. Eventually, the soup is as cool as the air. When there is no longer any energy difference between the soup and air, nothing more happens.

Giant stars end their life with a huge explosion, or supernova, that produces huge amounts of heat. Eventually, all stars will end up as nothing but heat and the universe will become nothing but a featureless sea of heat.

LOSING ENERGY

You will need

- ✔ A Newton's cradle, or a row of marbles placed in a groove just touching each other
- ✔ A towel

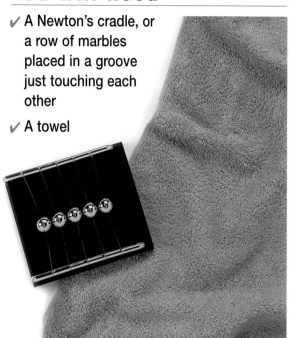

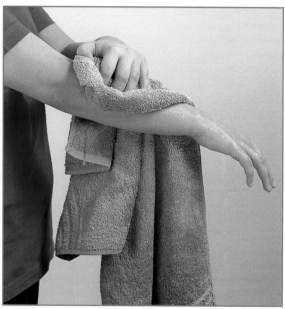

1 Dry yourself after bathing by dabbing with the towel. Now try rubbing the towel vigorously. Which way dries best?

In the real world

FRICTION

Moving things eventually slow down because of a force called friction—the force betweeen two things rubbing together. When two solids rub together, such as when a cup slides over a table, microscopic jagged edges on the surface of the cup and table snag. When a solid moves through air or water, the friction is countless collisions with air or water molecules. Friction makes things hot because as the friction slows the moving object down, its kinetic energy is converted to heat.

An ancient way to make fire was to spin a rod in a hole so that the friction generated heat.

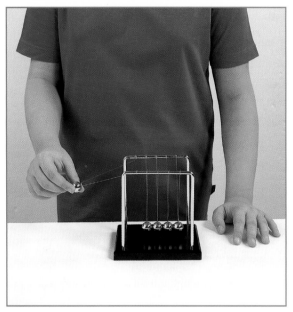

2 Pull up a ball at one end of a Newton's cradle to give it height and potential energy. Let the ball drop.

What is happening?

Whenever something moves, it loses some of its kinetic energy to its surroundings. At least some is lost as heat because of friction, the force between two things rubbing together. As friction slows things down, it converts the kinetic energy to heat. Rubbing with a towel dries better than dabbing because of the warmth generated by friction between towel and skin. Often, though, kinetic energy is lost more directly. Newton's cradle shows how this energy is not actually lost but simply passed on. One ball stops but another moves. But the balls will all eventually slow down and stop as more kinetic energy is lost as friction.

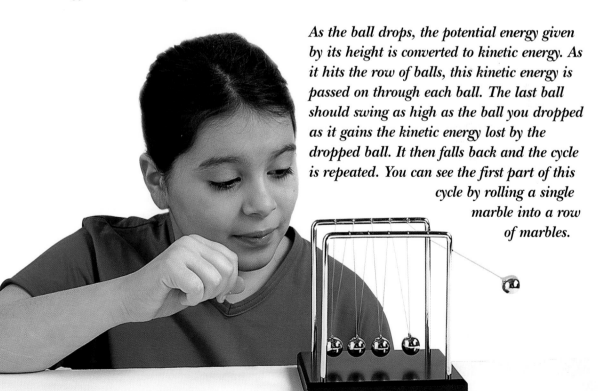

As the ball drops, the potential energy given by its height is converted to kinetic energy. As it hits the row of balls, this kinetic energy is passed on through each ball. The last ball should swing as high as the ball you dropped as it gains the kinetic energy lost by the dropped ball. It then falls back and the cycle is repeated. You can see the first part of this cycle by rolling a single marble into a row of marbles.

ENERGY SOURCES

The modern world demands huge amounts of energy. Plentiful energy is needed to give us warmth and light, and also for all the power to run cars, trains, aircraft, and every other kind of machine.

Over 99 percent of natural energy reaching the earth's surface comes from the Sun. Just a tiny fraction is heat from the earth's interior, called geothermal energy. An even smaller fraction is tidal energy

Watermills have taken energy from running water, cleanly and renewably, for centuries.

Did you know?

The average American uses 330 times as much energy as the average Ethiopian.

created by the pull of the Moon and Sun's gravity.

The Sun beams huge amounts of energy at the earth—about the same amount each year as 200 million power stations. A third is reflected back into space. Most of the remaining energy either warms the air or leaks back into space, or is used up in natural water circulation—evaporating water from the oceans and driving the weather. Plant leaves soak up about 0.06 percent of the Sun's energy to sustain their growth.

So very little of the Sun's energy is used directly. Solar energy cells that turn sunlight into electricity provide barely 0.01 percent of the world's energy needs.

Most energy comes from fossil fuels that occur naturally in the ground, either as a solid (coal), a liquid (oil), or a gas (natural gas). But all of these got their energy originally from the Sun. They are all the buried remains of plants and animals that lived in the sunshine millions of years ago.

Fossil fuels are burned to produce heat, which is either used directly in fires and furnaces, used to power engines, or used to heat steam to generate electricity. Fossil fuels take millions of years to replace, so they are said to be nonrenewable energy sources.

Nuclear energy (page 26) is also nonrenewable because it burns up uranium and plutonium fuel. But because it uses so little fuel, nuclear energy is said to be a sustainable energy source.

Less than 5 percent of the world's energy comes from what are called renewable sources like trees, running water, the waves, tides, and winds.

In the real world

FOSSIL FUELS

Each of the three fossil fuels—coal, oil, and natural gas—is created in a different way from the buried remains of plants and animals that lived millions of years ago. Coal is made from remains of plants that grew in huge swamps in the Carboniferous Period, 300 million years ago. Oil was formed from tiny plants and animals that lived in warm seas. As they died, they were buried under sea-bed mud. Heat and pressure underground turned them to oil. Vapors from the oil collect underground to form natural gas pockets.

Oil usually comes out of the ground as thick, black crude oil. It must then be refined to separate it into fuels like gasoline for trucks and kerosene for aircraft.

SOLAR ENERGY

You will need

- ✓ A length of aluminum foil
- ✓ Scissors
- ✓ A shoe box or pizza delivery box
- ✓ Adhesive tape
- ✓ Acetate or clear cellophane
- ✓ An egg for cooking

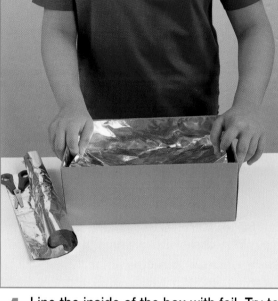

1 Line the inside of the box with foil. Try to keep the foil smooth and wrinkle-free. Cut a large window in the lid.

In focus

Curved mirrors focus sunlight on to the solar cell (at the top).

SOLAR ENERGY

Huge amounts of energy arrive on the earth each day in sunlight. This sunlight, or solar energy, can be collected and turned into electricity. Special units called solar cells produce a small burst of electricity when they are struck by photons (tiny packets) of sunlight. The more solar cells are linked together, the more power is produced. Small, flat arrays of solar cells are often used in small appliances such as calculators or to provide extra power for heating water for small buildings. But these flat arrays only produce small amounts of energy. To collect enough energy for power stations to supply towns, or for industrial use, the Sun's rays have to be concentrated by special curved mirrors that move round to track the Sun during the day.

What is happening?

Part of the sunlight reaching the earth is ultraviolet rays. Humans cannot see these rays, but they tan the skin. In too large doses, they can cause sunburn and even skin cancer. Sunlight also contains other invisible rays, called infrared rays. Infrared rays have a high heat content, and sun ray lamps for artificial tanning have a lot of infrared energy. The solar cooker in this experiment captures infrared rays from the Sun to fry the egg. The foil is needed to reflect the rays into the box and concentrate the Sun's energy. The cellophane window keeps the heat from escaping as it builds up inside the box.

2 Cut a piece of cellophane slightly larger than the window in the lid, and tape it into place on the underside of the lid.

You have now made a solar cooker. Put the lid on the box and place it outside in hot sunshine. Make sure the window is facing the Sun directly. If necessary, tilt the box so that the Sun shines right into the window. After half an hour or so the cooker should be hot enough to fry an egg inside.

HUMAN ENERGY

Like automobiles, human bodies need energy in the form of a fuel. The body does get a tiny amount of energy from the warmth of sunlight, but most of its energy comes from its own special fuel—food.

The body's main fuel is glucose, which is used to power every cell in the body. Glucose is a kind of sugar made by plants as they take energy from sunlight. The main process by which the body gets energy is called sugar metabolism. Glucose is common in many fruits and fruit juices, but most of the glucose used by the body comes from foods called carbohydrates. These are very common parts of all plant matter and are found in starchy food such as bread, cakes, and potatoes. The body cannot use

People need to eat every day to provide the food energy their bodies need to work.

these carbohydrates as energy directly. Instead they are broken down into glucose by the digestive system.

Glucose is either circulated in the blood and burned by the body directly, or temporarily stored in the liver and muscles as a chemical called glycogen. For the body to work effectively, levels of sugar in the blood must always be just right. So the

Did you know?

The human body turns chemical energy into heat. A classroom of 10 children creates about the same amount of heat as a 1-kilowatt electric fire.

Human bodies produce a surprising amount of heat energy.

body has two special hormones called glucagon and insulin to keep the levels controlled. In people suffering from diabetes, this control mechanism fails.

Weight for weight, foods called fats are twice as rich in energy as carbohydrates. Fats are found in many foods such as butter and cheese. They are harder for the body to use, but because fats can give more energy than carbohydrates for the same weight, they are easier to carry around. So the body stores fats in different places to provide extra supplies in times of food shortage.

Besides carbohydrates and fats, foods called proteins are also used by the body for energy. But protein has many other uses in the body and is only used as an energy source in emergencies.

NUCLEAR ENERGY

Despite the tiny size of an atom, a great deal of energy is needed to bind together its nucleus, or core. Each nucleus is made up of pure energy. By releasing some of this energy from millions of atomic nuclei, nuclear power stations produce a great deal of energy from just a few tons of nuclear fuel. Nuclear bombs get their awesome destructive power the same way.

Like oil- and coal-fired power stations, nuclear power stations heat water to make steam to drive turbines that generate electricity. Nuclear power

Nuclear bombs are the most terrifying weapons ever created. Some, called atom bombs, get their energy from nuclear fission. Much more powerful hydrogen bombs work by fusing atoms of hydrogen.

Did you know?

Nuclear fuel is very concentrated. Little more than 6 lbs (about 3 kg) of uranium fuel provides enough energy to supply electricity to a city of one million people for an entire day.

stations get heat by splitting the nuclei of large atoms such as uranium. This is called nuclear fission; fission is another word for splitting.

Unfortunately, nuclear fission produces not only energy but also dangerous radiation. So scientists one day hope to produce power by nuclear fusion—that is, by fusing nuclei together instead. This is what happens in the heart of every star, including the Sun.

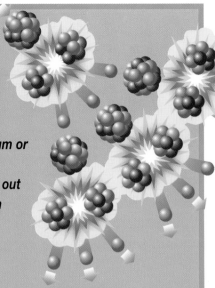

In focus

The chain reaction is started by firing neutrons (blue balls) at a nucleus of uranium or plutonium. When the nucleus splits, it fires out more neutrons, which split more nuclei in a chain reaction.

NUCLEAR CHAIN REACTION

In nuclear fission, the nuclei of atoms are split by firing neutrons at them. Neutrons are tiny particles from inside nuclei. So when neutrons crash into a nucleus and split it, they release some more neutrons. These neutrons then shoot out in all directions, and split other nuclei. As these nuclei split, they shoot out still more neutrons to split nuclei. So the whole process gathers pace in what is called a chain reaction, until all the nuclei are split.

When an atom is split, it releases huge amounts of energy. The bigger the atom, the more energy is released. In a nuclear bomb, millions of nuclei are split in a fraction of a second in a chain reaction, creating an explosion.

In nuclear power stations, special control rods are used to slow the chain reaction down so that the energy is released gradually over a long period. The rods absorb neutrons before they split other nuclei.

ALTERNATIVE ENERGY

Developed parts of the world like the United States and Europe already use colossal amounts of energy, and energy consumption is rising rapidly elsewhere in the world.

With such heavy demand, the world's supply of fossil fuels may soon run out. It is thought that the world's oil reserves could be completely used up in less than half a century. Even coal supplies could last little more than 170 years. Moreover, the use of such huge amounts of

fossil fuels is harming the environment. Burning fossil fuels not only pollutes the atmosphere with soot; it also pumps huge amounts of carbon dioxide gas into the air. The excess of carbon dioxide traps much more of the Sun's heat than is natural and so is making the entire world warm up. This is called global warming.

Because of these problems, many people believe we should develop alternative sources of energy that generate electricity

In focus

HYDROELECTRIC POWER

Hydroelectric power relies on falling water to turn the turbines that generate electricity. Dams are often constructed to build up a good head or pressure

of deep water. The power station is set inside the base of the dam, where the pressure is greatest. Sluice gates open to let the water gush through tunnels and onto the turbines.

Hells Canyon Dam on the Snake River in Idaho.

more cleanly and are renewable —that is, they are continually restocked. Running water (hydroelectric power or HEP), wind, waves, tides, and heat from the Sun (solar power) and the earth's interior (geothermal power) are all renewable.

Wind power uses giant, wind-driven turbines to turn electricity generators. Wave power generates electricity with floating booms that are rocked by the waves. Tidal power uses the sea falling from a high tide to turn generators.

Of these, only HEP is widely used, providing a fifth of the world's electricity. HEP power stations are expensive to build. They often involve building huge dams, which can destroy farmland and natural habitats. But once working, they are very cheap to run and produce inexhaustible, clean energy.

Powerful wind turbines at Delaware Mountain in Texas.

Experiments in Science

Science is about knowledge: it is concerned with knowing and trying to understand the world around us. The word comes from the Latin word, *scire*, to know.

In the early 17th century, the great English thinker Francis Bacon suggested that the best way to learn about the world was not simply to think about it, but to go out and look for yourself—to make observations and try things out. Ever since then, scientists have tried to approach their work with a mixture of observation and experiment. Scientists insist that an idea or theory must be tested by observation and experiment before it is widely accepted.

All the experiments in this book have been tried before, and the theories behind them are widely accepted. But that is no reason why you should accept them. Once you have done all the experiments in this book, you will know the ideas are true not because we have told you so, but because you have seen for yourself.

All too often in science there is an external factor interfering with the result which the scientist just has not thought of. Sometimes this can make the experiment seem to work when it has not, as well as making it fail. One scientist conducted lots of demonstrations to show that a clever horse called Hans could count things and tap out the answer with his hoof. The horse was indeed clever, but later it was found that rather than counting, he was getting clues from tiny unconscious movements of the scientist's eyebrows.

This is why it is very important when conducting experiments to be as rigorous as you possibly can. The more casual you are, the more "eyebrow factors" you will let in. There will always be some things that you cannot control. But the more precise you are, the less these are likely to affect the outcome.

What went wrong?

However careful you are, your experiments may not work. If so, you should try to find out where you went wrong. Then repeat the experiment until you are absolutely sure you are doing everything right. Scientists learn as much, if not more, from experiments that go wrong as those that succeed. In 1929, Alexander Fleming discovered the first antibiotic drug, penicillin, when he noticed that a bacteria culture he was growing for an experiment had gone moldy—and that the mold seemed to kill the bacteria. A poor scientist would probably have thrown the moldy culture away. A good scientist is one who looks for alternative explanations for unexpected results.

Glossary

alternative energy: Energy from a source other than coal, oil, gas, or nuclear.

calorie: Measure of food energy: the heat needed to warm 1 kg of water by 1°C.

calorimeter: Device for measuring the heat energy produced when something burns or changes.

conservation, energy: How the total energy stays the same before and after every transformation.

fission, nuclear: The way nuclear energy is released in nuclear power stations by splitting the nuclei of large atoms such as uranium.

fossil fuel: Oil, coal, or natural gas extracted from the ground. All are fuels made over millions of years from the remains of plants and animals.

fusion, nuclear: The way nuclear energy is released in nuclear bombs and in stars by fusing (joining) the nuclei of small atoms such as hydrogen.

heat engine: Device that burns a fuel to produce movement, converting stored energy to heat energy then mechanical energy.

inertia: Natural tendency of things to stay still until they are forced to move.

joule: The amount of energy needed to lift one pound weight nine inches upward. One joule is equal to 0.042 food calories.

kinetic energy: The energy due to movement.

momentum: Natural tendency of things to stay moving at the same speed in the same direction until they are forced to change.

neutron: One of the two kinds of particles in the nucleus of an atom. Neutrons are used to split nuclei in nuclear fission.

nonrenewable energy: Energy sources such as coal and oil which take nature millions of years to create—so supplies will eventually be used up.

nucleus: The central cluster of protons and neutrons in an atom.

photosynthesis: The process by which plant leaves convert the energy in sunlight into stored, chemical energy.

potential energy: Stored energy, ready to make something happen.

renewable energy: Energy from a source that is quickly replenished, like the wind, or effectively limitless, like sunlight.

thermodynamics: The science of heat movement.

transfer, energy: The movement of energy from one place to another.

transformation, energy: The change of energy from one form to another.

work: How much something moves when energy is transferred from one place to another.

Index

A

archery 8
atom 4-5, 26-27

C

calories 24
calorimeter 5
carbohydrates 24-25
carbon dioxide 28
coal 13, 21
Conservation of Energy law 16

D, E

dams 28-29
diabetes 25
electricity 5, 7, 13, 21-22, 26, 28-29

F

fats 25
food 24-25
fossil fuels 21, 28
friction 18-19

G, H

geothermal energy 20, 29
global warming 28
glucose 24-25
gravity 7, 9-10, 21
heat 4-5, 7, 14-19, 21, 23-25, 28
heat engines 14-17
hydroelectric power 28-29

I, J, K

infrared rays 23
joule 4-5
kinetic energy 6-11, 19

N

neutrons 27
nuclear energy 5, 21, 26-27
nuclear fission 27
nuclear fusion 27
nucleus 26-27

O

oil 21

P

photosynthesis 12
potential energy 6-11, 19
proteins 25

S

solar energy 5, 12, 21-22, 29
stars 4, 17, 27
steam 13-15, 21, 26

T, U

temperature 17
thermodynamics 16
tidal energy 20
ultraviolet rays 23